Mystical Creatures of Korea: Strange and Beautiful Tales from Folklore

Soojin Kim

Mystical Creatures of Korea:
Strange and Beautiful Tales from Folklore

In Korea, many mysterious creatures and characters have been passed down through stories, folklore, and fairy tales. I hope this book will give you a chance to get a little more familiar with them.

From the author: someone who spent their childhood completely lost in over 100 Korean fairy tales.

Contents

Tiger

The tiger is the king of the mountains. Long ago, many tigers lived in the mountains of Korea. People were a little scared of them, but they also respected the tiger as a symbol of power and dignity.

The tiger who was afraid of dried persimmon

One hungry tiger wandered down to a village one night, its belly rumbling loudly. Peeking into a small house, it heard a baby crying. The mother said, "Stop crying, or the tiger will come and take you away." But the baby only cried louder. Quickly, the mother offered something sweet, saying softly, "Here is a gotgam (dried persimmon), shhh..."

The tiger, hiding outside, listened carefully. It didn't know what a gotgam was, or what it looked like, but to its surprise, the baby stopped crying right away. "Gotgam...? What is that?" the tiger

1

whispered to itself. "It stopped the baby crying, but the baby isn't even afraid of me!" Just then, a thief hiding on the roof slipped and fell right onto the tiger's back. "Ouch!" he cried. The tiger, thinking it was the terrifying gotgam jumping on him, bolted back into the mountains, trembling with fear. From that day on, people say tigers would shiver at the sound of the word "gotgam."

Did You Know?
In the 17th century, there were about 6,000 tigers in Korea! But their numbers slowly dropped, and during the Japanese colonial period, there was a big tiger hunt. Now, tigers are extinct on the Korean Peninsula.

Magpie

Magpies have been loved by Koreans for a long time because they are a symbol of good luck! People believed that when a magpie chirped in the morning, it meant good news or a special guest would come. There's even a children's song: "Yesterday was the magpie's New Year, and today is ours!"

The magpie that repaid a kindness

Long ago, a scholar was walking along a path when he heard loud, noisy chirps. Looking up, he saw a nest of baby magpies and noticed a big snake about to swallow them! Quickly, he drew his bow and shot the snake, saving the little birds. The mother magpie flew around him in thanks, chirping happily.

That night, the scholar lost his way and found an old house with a tall bell tower. A beautiful woman living there offered him food and a place to sleep. As he slept, a sharp cry woke him up. A magpie was bravely pecking at a big snake that was about to attack him. When the scholar looked closely, he was surprised to see that the snake was the very same woman he had met before. The snake's mate had been killed by the scholar that day, and she wanted revenge. The scholar shot an arrow and chased the snake away, but the magpie was already hurt very badly. Soon, the magpie died. The sad scholar buried it in a warm, sunny place. People later called it "the magpie that repaid kindness," and the story was passed down for many generations.

Did You Know?
While magpies are considered lucky in Korea, crows are seen as unlucky.

Heavenly Maiden

Heavenly Maidens are beautiful women who serve the King of Heaven, the Jade Emperor. You can think of them a bit like angels. They wear special feathered clothes that let them fly between the sky and the land. There's even a children's song that says, when *it snows, the Heavenly Maidens sprinkle snowflakes from the sky.*

The Heavenly Maiden and the Woodcutter

In a village in the mountains, there lived a woodcutter. He was very lonely and often felt sorry for himself.

One day, he saved a deer that was running away from a hunter. The deer wanted to thank him and led him to a small waterfall. This was a secret place where Heavenly Maidens came down from the sky to bathe. The deer whispered that if he hid one of the maidens' robes, good fortune would come to him.

The woodcutter sneaked and quickly took one of the maidens' feathered clothes and hid it. When the maidens finished bathing, the one whose clothes were missing couldn't fly back to heaven with the others. She stayed behind and sobbed.

The woodcutter pretended not to know anything. He went to her and asked, "Do you need my help?" Then he took her back to his house.

Thinking she had lost her feathered clothes forever, the maiden eventually fell in love with the woodcutter. They lived happily and had three children together.

One day, the maiden found her hidden feathered clothes in a drawer. She put on her clothes, took her three children, and flap-flap, up into the sky she flew!

When the woodcutter realized what had happened, he cried and cried—*sob-sob!*—but they never came back. People say the woodcutter then turned into a rooster and would often look up at the sky and cry "cock-a-doodle-doo!"

Did You Know?
Although heavenly maidens lived in the heavens, people believed that they often came down to bathe in clear natural places on earth like waterfalls, ponds, and mountain streams. This was because people thought such places were sacred.

Mountain Spirit

The Mountain Spirit is a mysterious being who lives deep in the mountains. They are magical and powerful, and sometimes people call them a "wise immortal."

The Golden Axe and the Silver Axe

Once upon a time, an honest woodcutter lived in the mountains. One day, as he was chopping wood by a pond—*chop-chop!*—his hands slipped, and his iron axe fell into the water.

"Oh no! What am I going to do? I can't work without my axe!" he cried.

Just then, the Mountain Spirit appeared from the pond—*splash!*—holding a golden axe and a silver axe. The Mountain Spirit held out the golden axe and asked,

"Is this axe yours?"

The woodcutter shook his head, "No."

8

Next, the Mountain Spirit held out the silver axe and asked,

"Is this one yours?"

The woodcutter shook his head no again.

Then the Mountain Spirit laughed—*Ha-ha-ha!*—and said,

"You are a truly honest person! I will give you the golden axe, the silver axe, and your iron axe too!"

The woodcutter was so happy to receive all three axes. He sold the golden and silver axes and became very rich.

Did You Know?
Long ago, people performed ceremonies for the Mountain Spirit. They would offer things like rice wine on top of a mountain to show respect.

Dokkaebi

The Dokkaebi is one of the most famous creatures in Korean stories. Goblins usually have two horns and sharp teeth, yet they look a bit like humans. They carry a magic club that can make gold and silver appear. Long ago, people would sometimes see a strange light over a graveyard and call it Dokkaebi's fireball, believing it was the magic of a Dokkaebi.

The magic club

One day, a kind but poor young man found a special hazelnut while walking through his village. He carefully put it in his pocket to give to his parents later. But he got lost in the forest and came across an old, big house. Inside, a group of Dokkaebi were having a noisy party, tapping their magic clubs on the floor and shouting, "Come out, gold, ttukttak! Come out, silver, ttukttak!" Just like that, gold and silver treasures appeared from the clubs. The young man hid in a storage room and watched them.

After a while, he got very hungry and bit into the hazelnut. "Snap!" The sound was so loud that the Dokkaebi panicked. "What was that sound? Is the house falling down?" they cried. Scared, they threw their magic clubs on the floor and ran away. When the house was empty, the young man quietly picked up one of the magic club. After he went back home, he did exactly what the Dokkaebi had done, and gold and silver treasures appeared! He became very rich.

His greedy neighbor heard about the sudden fortune and wanted the same magic. He took a hazelnut and went to the Dokkaebi's house, hiding in the same storage room. When night came, the Dokkaebi arrived and began their party. The neighbor bit into the hazelnut, and "Snap!" The Dokkaebi froze. "That's him!" they shouted, and they chased the neighbor out, beating him with their clubs. In the end, he went home empty-handed, learning a lesson the hard way.

Did You Know?
Usually, Korean goblins are called Dokkaebi. In old stories, they were imagined as scary monsters with horns and big bodies. But in modern times, like in the popular Korean drama *Dokkaebi*, they are sometimes shown as handsome, clever men.

Jangseung

Jangseung are special wooden guardian posts that protect villages. They are usually set up at the village entrance. When there is a pair—a male and a female—they are called the Great General of the Sky and the Great Female General of the Land.

The Jangseung Trial

Long ago, a tall Jangseung stood at the entrance of every village, like a giant Korean totem pole. One day, a silk merchant leaned against a Jangseung to rest and fell fast asleep. But when he woke up, his precious silk was gone!

The merchant hurried to the town's magistrate to find the thief. The clever magistrate made a plan.
"That Jangseung is the thief!" he shouted. "Bring it to me!"

The puzzled officers pulled up the Jangseung and carried it to the magistrate.

"Beat the Jangseung!" The magistrate commanded. When villagers heard that a Jangseung was being beaten like a criminal, they all came running to watch. The magistrate looked at them and said firmly, "It is wrong for people to crowd and disturb a trial. Each of you must pay a roll of silk as a fine."
One by one, the villagers handed over their silk. Among the rolls, the magistrate spotted the missing silk and caught the real thief.

Did You Know?
In Korea, many villages were named Jangseungbaegi, which means "a place where a Jangseung stood."

Dragon

The word "Yong" is used for both Western and Eastern dragons in Korea, but they look very different!

The dragon in Korean stories has a long, wiggly body like a snake, horns like a deer, and shiny scales like a fish. A dragon can fly and is a symbol of wisdom and power, often representing the king.

The Golden Dragon's Request

Long ago, near a quiet village, there was a wide, dry wasteland. In that village lived a brave warrior who was very good with a bow and arrow. One night, a golden dragon appeared in his dream and pleaded,

"Tomorrow I will fight a blue dragon. Please shoot the blue dragon with your bow, and I will reward you."

The next day, the warrior went outside and saw the golden dragon and the blue dragon locked together in a fierce battle!

He aimed carefully, just as the golden dragon had asked, and shot the blue dragon. The arrow struck true, and the blue dragon fell.

Grateful, the golden dragon filled the dry wasteland with sparkling water. The land turned rich and green, and the warrior became very wealthy.

Did You Know?
During the Joseon Dynasty, the king's face was called Yong-an, which means "the face of a dragon."
People used this special phrase to show great respect when speaking of the king.

Yongwang

Just as the Jade Emperor rules the sky, yongwang rules the sea! He lives in a beautiful palace under the water.

The Rabbit and the Turtle

The yongwang had a loyal follower, a turtle. One day, the yongwang became very sick. His doctor said he needs the liver of a land animal—a rabbit!

"Go to the land and get a rabbit's liver for me," the yongwang ordered.
The turtle immediately went to the shore and found a rabbit. But to trick the rabbit, he told a lie:
"I've heard you are very quick and smart," said the turtle.
"Our King wants to invite you to his palace under the sea, to give you a feast and praise you!"

The proud rabbit followed the turtle into the sea.

17

But when he arrived, he realized the yongwang wanted to eat his liver!

"If you need my liver, I'd be happy to give it, Your Majesty! But oh— rabbits can take their livers in and out. I left mine in a tree! If the turtle had told me, I would have brought it."

The yongwang and turtle believed him and took him back to land.

"Hurry up and get your liver," the turtle said. But the rabbit just laughed. "How can I take my liver out of my body? This is your punishment for tricking me!"

The rabbit hopped away into the forest, laughing, while the turtle was full of regret. But it was too late.

Did You Know?

Long ago, when sailors were at sea and a storm came, they thought the yongwang was angry. To calm him, they would throw offerings into the water or perform a special ceremony.

Princess Bari

Princess Bari, also called Baridegi, is a brave heroine from Korean shamanism. She saved her parents and became a legendary figure across Korea.

The Story of Princess Bari

Long ago, there was a king who had a big worry: his first six children were all daughters. Since only a son could become king, he desperately hoped his next child would be a boy. But his seventh child was another girl! Disappointed, the king ordered that his youngest daughter be abandoned. Because she was discarded, people called her Baridegi, which means "discarded."

Time passed. The king became very sick, and the doctors said only a special medicinal water from the Underworld could cure him. He asked his daughters who would go fetch the water, but the first six daughters all shook their heads. Then the queen went to find Baridegi. When Baridegi heard what had happened, she immediately promised, "I will go and get the water!"

Wearing iron shoes and carrying an iron staff, Baridegi began her long, difficult journey. After a long time, she finally reached the medicinal spring in the Underworld. But an armed monk guarded the spring and would not give her the water easily. Baridegi followed his instructions: she became his wife and gave birth to seven sons. Only then did the monk give her the medicinal water.

Baridegi returned home with the water, her husband, and her seven sons. Both the king and queen had already died. She poured the water into the mouths of her parents and the king and queen came back to life! They were overjoyed and thanked Baridegi for her courage, kindness, and determination. After that, Baridegi became a goddess who guides the souls of the dead to paradise, leading them on the path to the afterlife and serving as the first guardian spirit for shamans.

Did You Know?
The legend of Princess Bari has over 100 different versions across Korea! Each region has its own unique story, characters, and details.

Do-sa

A Do-sa is a magical person who can do amazing tricks and skills. You could think of them as a mix between a ninja and a superhero! One of the most famous Do-sa was a man named Jeon Woo-chi. He really lived in history, but over time, lots of magical stories were added to his legend. In the tales, Jeon Woo-chi used his magic to help the poor by tricking the king's treasury. You could even call him Korea's Robin Hood!

Do-sa Jeon Woo-chi

A long time ago, there lived a very clever man named Jeon Woo-chi. One day, he learned some magical powers, but he kept them a secret. When he saw that poor villagers were hungry, he decided he had to help them. He disguised himself as a heavenly official from the Jade Emperor and appeared before the king, floating on a cloud.

"Your Majesty," said Jeon Woo-chi, "I bring a message from the Jade Emperor! You must build a golden ridgepole for our palace!" The king trembled and quickly obeyed. He made a golden ridgepole and gave it to Jeon Woo-chi. Then Jeon Woo-chi sold the ridgepole, bought lots of grain, and shared it with all the hungry villagers.

When the king and his officials realized they had been tricked, they tried to catch Jeon Woo-chi. But *poof!*—he disappeared using his magic. From that day on, Jeon Woo-chi used his powers to fight bad guys and help the weak.

Did You Know?
Another famous Korean hero is Hong Gil-dong! He was also a "righteous thief" who used clever tricks and magic. But while Hong Gil-dong was completely fictional, Jeon Woo-chi was a real person who became a hero through his cleverness and trick.

Haetae

A Haetae is a magical creature that looks a lot like a lion but has horns. People say it can tell right from wrong and stop disasters like fires. In old times, statues of Haetae were placed at the entrances of palaces to protect them. It is also called a Haechi.

The crying Haetae

During the Joseon Dynasty, a government official was punished for a crime he did not commit. That night, a strange, loud "Waaaah!" was heard all the way to the palace. The king was scared and ordered his officials to find out what was happening.

The guards saw the Haetae statue at the front gate suddenly stretch and stand up, crying "Waaaah! Waaaah!" They were so frightened that they ran away.

The next day, the officials talked about the crying Haetae. One said, "Maybe the Haetae is trying to tell us something!" They checked the case again and discovered that the official had been wrongly accused. He was allowed to return, and after that, the Haetae's loud cries were never heard again.

Did You Know?
In Korea, you can see Haetae statues guarding important places like Gwanghwamun Gate, Gyeongbokgung Palace, and the National Assembly Building!

Bulgasari

A Bulgasari is a strange and magical monster that grows bigger and stronger by eating metal. People called it "Bulgasari," which means "unkillable," because no one could ever destroy it. Usually, it stayed hidden in the mountains so people wouldn't see it, but it always watched over the village in secret.

The Bulgasari who swallowed fire

A long time ago, a strange creature called the Bulgasari appeared in a village. At first, the Bulgasari was very tiny. It grew bigger by eating little grains of rice given by a kind child. But soon, it began to swallow everything in its path, even pieces of metal. The villagers were frightened and tried to stop the Bulgasari, but its body was made of iron, and nothing could harm it.

Finally, the Bulgasari had to hide deep in the forest, away from the frightened villagers.

One hot summer day, a huge fire suddenly broke out in a village. The flames roared "Whoooosh!" and climbed high into the sky. Villagers ran around, shouting "Grab the water! Hurry!" and splashing buckets everywhere, but the fire only grew hotter and louder. Smoke filled the air, and sparks flew like tiny fireworks, "Pop! Crackle! Fwoosh!" The villagers were terrified, thinking the fire would never stop.

Just then, from the edge of the forest, a shiny, metal-covered creature appeared. It was the Bulgasari! Its eyes glimmered, and it opened its huge mouth with a mighty "Chomp! Chomp!" The Bulgasari began swallowing the fire, gulping up the flames, sparks, and smoke. The villagers watched in awe as the roaring fire slowly got smaller. The Bulgasari twisted and turned, gobbling up the fire with a "Snap! Crunch! Gulp!" The once scary flames shrank and hissed,

"Ssshh!", until the village was safe and smoke-free.

The villagers cheered and clapped. "Hooray for the Bulgasari!" they shouted. No longer afraid, they danced around and thanked the brave creature. From that day on, they carved the shape of the Bulgasari on their houses as a guardian, believing it would protect them from fire forever.

Did You Know?
The name "Bulgasari" is also used for a starfish in Korean! Just like the monster, a starfish can grow its arms back if they get cut off.

Bonghwang

The Bonghwang is a magical bird from ancient legends. People say it is a sacred creature, with rainbow-colored feathers that shine like jewels. In Korea's Joseon Dynasty, it became a symbol of nobility and holiness, a bit like the phoenix from Western stories.

The bird that stopped the drought

One year, a terrible drought hit the country. The fields were dry, the rivers were empty, and the people were sad. "Oh no! What will we do?" they cried. The King was filled with worry. He tried everything: he held rain ceremonies and tried to bring water from far away, but the water quickly dried up and nothing seemed to work. The King cried out sadly, "All of this is because I, the King, am not good enough!"

The King declared that he would not eat while his people starved, and he stopped eating. His officials knelt down and cried loudly, "Please save your body, Your Majesty!"

The King did not listen. He stopped eating and drinking, and he grew thinner and weaker. The King was nearly eighty years old and could feel his life slipping away. But still, the rain did not come.

One day, the King felt that his last breath was near. He thought that when he went to the heaven, he would meet the Jade Emperor and beg him to look down on his poor people and send rain. Thinking this, he felt happy and was no longer afraid to close his eyes.

Just then, high in the sky, a beautiful, magical bird appeared. It had a long, rainbow-colored tail that sparkled in the sunlight. It was the legendary Bonghwang!

The Bonghwang flew over the dry land, flapping its wings with a "Flap! Flap! Swish!" sound, and let out a sorrowful cry, "Kreeee! Kreeee!" Suddenly, dark clouds rolled in, rumbling "Grrrrumble! Pitter-pat!" and rain began to fall, soaking the fields and filling the rivers. The people jumped and danced with joy, shouting "Hooray!" The King was so happy he cried tears of thanks. He bowed deeply to the Bonghwang.

From then on, whenever a great disaster threatened the land, the Bonghwang would appear, cry with its beautiful voice, and then return to the sky.

Did You Know?
During the Joseon Dynasty, princesses and other royal women had clothes decorated with Bonghwang designs. This showed their high status, royal power, and the values of harmony and virtue.

Gumiho

A Gumiho is a magical fox with nine tails. It can use magic to change into a beautiful woman, but deep down, it dreams of living as a regular human.

The Gumiho's wish

One day, the Gumiho, disguised as a kind woman, found a woodcutter in the mountains. He had hurt his leg and was limping along the path. The Gumiho carefully gathered herbs, made medicine, and gently cared for him. "Thank you," the woodcutter said as he slowly healed. The Gumiho swished her tails from beneath her skirt, moving them with excitement.

After helping him, the Gumiho fell in love with the woodcutter. But she felt a little sad, for she was still a fox and not truly human. Her greatest dream was to become a regular human and live an ordinary life. Every dawn, the Gumiho climbed to the mountaintop to pray.

The Mountain Spirit, seeing the Gumiho's pure heart, felt sorry for her and said,

"I will give you nine trials. For every one you pass, I will take away one of your tails."

The Gumiho bowed her head and said she was ready to do anything.

The Mountain Spirit gave the Gumiho trials about honesty, mercy, self-control, friendship, gratitude, courage, sacrifice, and forgiveness. She could pass them only with a kind heart, care for others, and a willingness to sacrifice herself. Sometimes the trials tested her Gumiho instincts, but thinking only of the woodcutter, she quietly passed them all.

She managed to get rid of eight tails, and the last, ninth trial was about love. The Mountain Spirit said, "Now you have only one tail left. You know that regular Gumihos must eat one thousand human livers to become human, right?"

"Yes, Great Spirit. I am only thankful that you gave me these trials instead of forcing me to eat human livers."

"Haha. It is too early to be thankful. No matter how much I want to make you human, a Gumiho must eat a human liver to finally become human. I will give you one chance because of all your hard work. You only need the liver of that woodcutter next to you. If you eat it, I will instantly turn you into a human."

The Gumiho was shocked. "How can Heaven be so cruel? Is that the last trial?"

The path down the mountain was dark because the sun had not fully risen. The Gumiho ran right into the woodcutter, who was just heading out to chop wood. The woodcutter, completely unaware of her worry, greeted her with a bright smile. "Are you coming back from praying to the Mountain Spirit again?"

The Gumiho stared at the woodcutter. For hundreds of years, she had resisted eating human livers.

Even though she loved humans, the memories of being an outcast and having to hide after people discovered she was a monster rushed back. The Mountain Spirit's promise—that one single bite would make her human—crept into her mind. The tips of her ears slowly sharpened into fox-like points.

Just then, the woodcutter said, "It's dangerous in the mountains with the wild animals. Next time, come after the sun is fully up. Or better yet, come with me." The woodcutter laughed shyly.

His smile snapped the Gumiho back to reality. She was so ashamed that she had even for a second let her monster instincts think about hurting the person she loved. The Gumiho ran away deep into the mountain, fleeing from the woodcutter. She went so deep that no one could follow. There she sat and cried, and cried.

"Mountain Spirit! Mountain Spirit!" she cried out into the air. "I cannot do it! I would rather hide

in these deep mountains and live my life as a monster than eat his liver!"
Only the sound of her crying echoed through the deep mountains.

She cried for a long time, until a full day had passed and night fell again. Suddenly, the soft voice of the Mountain Spirit came to her. "Gumiho," he called, "Gumiho."

She weakly lifted her head, and the Mountain Spirit stood before her. "Great Spirit!" The Gumiho quickly knelt down. The Mountain Spirit said, "I now truly know your good heart. You have passed the final test." He swung his wooden staff, and the Gumiho's last tail vanished.

The Gumiho bowed again and again to Heaven with a joyful heart, then returned to the village. The Gumiho, now fully human, lived happily with the woodcutter, and they continued to be kind to all their neighbors.

Did You Know?

In old Korean folktales, the Gumiho often appears as a scary monster! The idea that it needs to eat the livers of animals or people to become human is a basic part of the stories.

The Messenger from the Underworld (Jeoseungsaja)

The Jeoseungsaja is a mysterious guide who calls the names of people whose time has come and takes them to the Heaven.

Take me instead!

In a small village, a kind grandmother lived with her young grandson. She had raised him all alone after his parents passed away in a tragic accident. The grandson loved his grandmother dearly and always tried to be good.

One day, as the grandson returned from the village, he saw a figure standing quietly in front of his grandmother. The figure wore a black hat and a flowing black robe. His grandmother was fast asleep on the porch. As the grandson stepped closer, the pale face of the figure turned toward him. "Ah! It's the Jeoseungsaja!" he thought, and he fell to his knees. "Please! Don't take my grandmother yet! Take me instead! I'll go in her place!" he cried, his voice shaking with fear.

Hearing her grandson's cries, the grandmother woke up with a start. She stood in front of him, her hands trembling but her eyes strong. "No, my dear child! I am old. It is my turn. Come, take me! I am ready!"

The Jeoseungsaja looked at the two, seeing their love and courage. He shook his head slowly, a sad sigh escaping him. "I have seen many beg to live, but never beg to die for another. I will come back another time," he said, and disappeared into the shadows.

The grandmother and grandson told everyone they knew about meeting the Messenger from the Underworld, but no one believed them. They were just thankful for the extra time they had been given.

They spent the next few decades doing good deeds for everyone around them.

The grandmother lived to be over 110 years old. On the day she turned 111, the Messenger from the Underworld appeared again. He looked exactly the same as before.

The Messenger said, "This should be enough, right?"

The grandmother nodded and willingly followed the Messenger.

Meanwhile, the grandson lived on to see his own children, their spouses, and even his grandchildren. When it was his turn, he was guided to the sky by the same Messenger from the Underworld and was reunited with his beloved grandmother.

Did You Know?

The Jeoseungsaja, who stood out in the film *K-pop Demon Hunters*! They are often shown wearing a black hat and robe because of a Korean TV series called *Hometown of Legends*. In older stories, there were no details about what they wore.

Jade Emperor (Okhwang-sangje)

The Jade Emperor is the king who rules the sky. He is the most powerful of all the heavenly spirits.

Gyeon-u and Jiknyeo

In a small village, a kind cowherd named Gyeon-u lived a simple life. Far above, in the heavens, a beautiful heavenly maiden named Jiknyeo watched over the land. One day, Jiknyeo came down by chance and saw Gyeon-u. Their eyes met, and instantly, they fell in love. Their heart fluttering like a bird.

When the Jade Emperor noticed that Jiknyeo had broken the rules to be with a human, he was very angry. "You must never meet again!" he thundered. Gyeon-u and Jiknyeo were heartbroken. Every day, they cried, their tears like tiny rivers.

Seeing their sorrow, the Jade Emperor softened a little. "Why do they cry so sadly? But a Heavenly Maiden and a human must not be together—it is the rule of the sky and the land. What can I do about this?"

As the Emperor was deep in thought, he noticed a crowd of crows sitting on a tree, crying. The Emperor clapped his hands together and said, "That's it! I will have the crows build a bridge so the two of them can meet in a place that is neither the sky nor the land!"

He decided they could meet just once a year. On the seventh day of the seventh month of the lunar calendar, he would order all the crows to build a bridge across the sky, so Gyeon-u and Jiknyeo could finally be together for one magical day.

Did You Know?

According to one folktale, after a human soul dies, it goes through many different Hell-courts for judgment. Finally, the soul arrives before the Jade Emperor. At that time, the Jade Emperor decides whether the soul will be reborn as a human or as an animal!

www.ingramcontent.com/pod-product-compliance
Lightning Source LLC
Chambersburg PA
CBHW051859090426
42811CB00003B/396